Under Par 'What I wish every golfer knew about golf'

Under Par 'What I wish every golfer knew about golf'

For Harvey Natalie and Lamorna.

SWING BUILDER

There are lots of illustrations, photographs and videos nowadays on the various media platforms available. I have chosen therefore not to include any visual material in this book. The aim is to provide golfers of all abilities a companion alongside his or her golfing journey. A 'go to' place to find suggestions and techniques to help to achieve game improvements. Very often a subtle change or adjustment can help to facilitate an improvement in any given area of your game. Also, I am confident that left handed players will be able read and understand the text from their own unique perspective. This is a game where it is very beneficial to have a positive thought process. By adopting this mind-set, 'I could can become I can'

SWING VISION

Your swing is reliable and consistent. This builds your confidence and you therefore quite naturally achieve better results.

Your posture feels comfortable and ready for action. Your stance promotes balance, relaxation and an athletic freedom of movement.

Your swing plane, governed by the angle of your spine, is ideal for you and suited to your physical characteristics. It is neither to upright, nor to flat, thus promoting the most natural, and energy efficient swing for you.

You develop a good rhythm as your arms work fluidly in cooperation with your turning body action, producing perfect timing into and through the golf ball. This is carried out at a tempo that is your tempo, the way you go about things.

Your alignment and the alignment of your swing, in relation to the target line, are in the optimum position to carry out the shot you see in your 'mind's eye'.

Your hold on the golf club (known as the grip), is placed on the club in such a way that enables the club face to be square to your chosen target line at address, and as you swing through the ball. Choosing a recognized best hold method is an essential factor in developing a sound swing action. **The term hold is preferred and used widely in this book.**

You are able to wind your trunk to enable you to make a full shoulder turn with your left shoulder (viewed from head on), from the 'three o'clock position to six o'clock' within your swing plane.

The angle of approach of the club head into the back of the golf ball is neither to steep, nor to shallow, as it sweeps through the ball.

Your swing is balanced, and has the ideal tempo (speed) suited to you and your natural personality. You release the controlled power you have naturally created, at exactly the right time coming into and through the ball.

You develop a pre-shot routine and a state of purposeful relaxation and concentration, stepping into the shot making process from assessment to completion. This is achieved by always keeping yourself in motion, from when you first imagine the shot to be played, through to the end of your pre-shot routine and completion of your swing. You have and stick to a standard routine that you can rely on, and trust, for every shot.

As you progress, through practice and actual play, you learn to feel and sense various aspects of the swing building process that help you feel what a good swing feels like for you. These can be used to great effect to help you to build a swing you can rely upon, especially under the pressure of competition.

When practicing, you do so thoughtfully. You take things one step at a time and build a rhythmic swing at your own tempo that you can trust. This gives you confidence in yourself to take out onto the golf course. With time, effort and determination, you develop the ability to imagine being on the golf course, feeling and rehearsing shots that you can then play during your next round. Also you can prepare and open up your mind to different strategies and approaches that you can subsequently take with you to the golf course.

You develop your own personal and comfortable warm up routine that you can use before practice and playing the golf course. This can involve stretching, practice swings, short putting and long putting (focusing mainly on distance control). Also focus on any key thoughts, actions or feelings that you want to include in your routines.

You develop an 'accepting resilience' mind-set. Remember, you can do no more than your best on each shot. You adopt a positive mind-set and vocabulary. Your expectation is that any external factor beyond your control can have an effect on your golf ball. This can be accepted and you can learn from these experiences. Faced with a similar situation again, you may choose a different strategy, but that is for a later time. You develop and integrate 'accepting resilience' into your way of thinking. This then immediately transports you into the present thus maintaining positive energy and momentum.

On the day of your game of golf, purposefully

slow things down, take thing steady and breathe. Determine to enjoy the day and give yourself time to get to the course and warm up. If you are playing your local course you will be well prepared, having prepared your strategy and rehearsed your round beforehand and by bringing along the clubs that you intend to utilise. Oh, and mark your golf ball to avoid any misunderstandings whilst out on the course, and remember your pitch repairer.

You take time to read the rules of golf. You can purchase a booklet that outlines the most frequent situations that you could encounter. You can carry this in your bag and use for reference purposes, which is very worthwhile and can save you shots out on the course.

EQUIPMENT

If you are new to the game of golf, you will be aware of a whole range of equipment available. This can appear quite daunting and expensive.

However in the early stages there are a number of options available to you in order to give the game a try. You could arrange tuition with your local professional, who can model and mentor for you just what can be achieved. This could incorporate a playing lesson over a few holes, where clubs could be provided. If a driving range is nearby you could hire a few clubs and give it a go. It could be that there are par three courses situated nearby that you could give a try.

If you get a feeling that this could be the game for you, then you can take steps to learn the basics, and develop your swing and other skills in order to make steady progress. This requires a thoughtful, methodical approach along with patience and persistence, as initial progress is steady. Slowly and surely is the way to approach your learning of this wonderful game.

If you decide that this is the game for you, there are a number of ways that you can obtain the equipment to play the game. Bear in mind though, that ladies clubs are usually shorter and lighter than for men, with smaller grips. Graphite shafts are predominant in the majority of ladies clubs, giving more flex and power to a slower swing speed. The more advanced lady golfer, with more strength and speed, can of course upgrade. You can invest in a second hand set of clubs, perhaps including a carry bag. You could go for a trolley, rather than electing to carry your clubs. You could source a half set either new or second hand. You can add a glove, balls, tees, a towel, a couple of pencils and a pitch repairer is a must!

As you progress, you can upgrade your equipment. This can include a better quality driver and other woods, utility clubs and irons. There are also a variety of wedges and putters, and power trolleys are also available. Ultimately, you can have clubs, including grips, fitted to your own personal specification.

Woods and utility woods are available with the club face at a variety of angles, and many golfers prefer these to long irons. Also the graphite shafts on the woods are made in a variety of flexes as follows: Extra Stiff, Stiff, Regular, Medium Mature (for seniors) and Ladies. It is desirable for the flex to be a good match to the swing speed you generate. This then gives you the best possible blend, in order to swing through the ball square to your target line, thus achieving better contact, better direction control and consistency. Generally the slower the swing the more loft is required on the face of a driver.

A graphite shaft has a kick point, which is the point in the shaft that bends the most during the swing. The range between the high and low kick point is around two inches. Most graphite shafts are made with the kick point around the middle of the range, as these can suit most players. A lower kick point can benefit a player, with a slower swing speed, to launch the ball into the air on a higher trajectory. A higher kick point can be very beneficial to a player who generates higher club head speed through the ball by achieving a lower more penetrating trajectory.

Putters can have different shaft lengths, be made of different materials, with various grip sizes. They are manufactured in all shapes and sizes, for example, the blade, the mallet and the peripheral weighted putter head. The face of the putter can be metal with or without an insert, and can also be grooved.

The blade will be toe down weighted. The mallet can be face balanced (around the shaft axis) and peripheral weighted, with markings on the top to aid alignment. A putter containing peripheral weighting, will normally have added weight in the heel and toe, which gives the putter added resistance to twisting at moment of impact with the golf ball (known as MOI, meaning Moment of Inertia).

A putter containing an insert, can increase MOI capability and start the ball rolling sooner on its journey, thus giving it better potential to hold the designated target line. A putter face containing grooves can also help to get the golf ball rolling smoothly off the face of the putter. The wider the grip, the less wrist action comes into play during the putting stroke. However this can also reduce feedback and your feel for the putt.

Irons can be forged 'muscle backs' (modern blades), or cast cavity backs (commonly known as 'game improvement clubs'). Cavity back irons are cast and designed in such a way that results in the weight behind the face, being distributed to the base and sides of the club. Hence the name cavity back. The benefits of using this type of club are that it is easier to launch the ball, and off-centre shots fair better in terms of travel and the desired direction of the golf ball. Muscle backs are normally forged with more material low down and behind the face. They are used by more advanced players, as they require a more precise contact through the ball to achieve the desired result. Also they give better feedback to the player, and they are more responsive when shaping shots. The lines between the two however, are not as distinct as they once were, with forged blades being designed to contain a shallow cavity to improve accuracy, and cavity back irons designed to allow the player to shape the ball with more feel. Iron club shafts can be made of steel or graphite, with a range of weight and flex options.

The composition of the golf ball has evolved over the years with two piece and multi-layer balls being available. They are designed to have different features, in terms of distance, the amount of spin generated and the amount of feel and feedback given to the player. Designers and manufacturers use technology to provide golf balls that meet the requirements of the golfer, from the high handicapper through to the scratch player. Costs range from a standard two piece ball, up to a more sophisticated multilayer ball which tends to be played by the more advanced player.

CHRISTOPHER PEAKE

There are various two-piece balls available, made primarily with distance in mind. They have a firmer outer layer of a material called surlyn, and also have higher compression, that in turn creates a greater velocity. However, this type of ball feels harder on the club face and spins less. Two piece balls with lower compression, and therefore a little softer, can benefit golfers with slower swing speeds to gain more distance.

Multilayer golf balls are softer than the two piece variety with some versions having a softer outer layer called urethane (similar to balata but more durable). This ball, with a urethane cover gives the more advanced player good feel and feedback together with good distance from well executed shots.

Take good care of to your golfing equipment, keep your clubs clean to get the best out of them, and if you play a lot remember to renew the grips on your clubs when required.

THE TARGET

When you have developed your swing technique, pre-shot routine and key thought processes, you can then rely and trust upon these out on the golf course. This then 'frees you up' to concentrate and apply your energy to sending the golf ball to your chosen target.

You look from behind the golf ball, concentrate and focus on your precise target. You adopt this as part of your pre-shot routine. You see, imagine and feel the shot that you want to achieve and where you desire your golf ball to come to rest.

You pick a site mark around a metre in front of the golf ball on your target line, for example a blade of grass or an indentation in the ground.

POSTURE

You move around to the side of the target line to address the golf ball and stand comfortably tall with your chin comfortably off your chest. Your feet are comfortably together and the golf ball is opposite the centre of your stance at this stage. Bend from your waist and your posterior will naturally and comfortably move out behind you. This also helps to set your spine at your correct natural angle for you.

Having bent from the waist, this allows your arms to just hang down naturally, and also allows the club head to sit in its natural position behind the golf ball (the way it was made to sit). Your feet are now quite naturally the correct distance from the golf ball, which will vary depending upon your height and the golf club you are using.

Your head will not be arched back at the neck so that you are looking down along your nose towards the golf ball. To do so is to create unnecessary tension in the base of the back of your neck. This will restrict and hinder the smooth motion of your swing. To avoid this, the back of your head is held comfortably in line with your back. Your eyes are then able to naturally move and focus on the back of the golf ball.

SWING PLANE

The taller you are then quite naturally the steeper your swing plane will be, so you will need to stand tall with your knees comfortably well flexed. This will automatically and naturally bring your head and hands higher and help to guard against a swing plane that is too steep. By achieving a flatter swing plane naturally by degrees, the club head will come into the golf ball more solidly and at a better angle.

The shorter you are the flatter your swing plane will quite naturally be, so you will need to stand with your legs comfortably straighter with less flex in the knees than a taller person would need. This will help you to guard against a swing plane that is to flat. By achieving a steeper swing plane naturally by degrees, the club head will come into the golf ball more solidly and at a better angle.

Your swing plane will quite naturally be flatter with you woods getting progressively steeper down through your irons to your wedges. Your hands however, will always be a similar distance from your thighs.

You will need to practice (preferably with a friend) and experiment thoughtfully to find the ideal swing plane for you.

To help you to picture a suitable swing plane in your imagination, you could model yourself on a professional player of your choice with a similar height and build to yourself.

ALIGNMENT

Place the club head behind the golf ball using your right hand, keeping your shoulders parallel to your chosen target line. The leading edge of the club face, is aligned precisely square to your chosen site mark, and therefore the target line and your target. More help on holding the golf club follows.

Next place your left hand on the golf club and comfortably form your hold. For a straight shot' your shoulders remain parallel to the target line, along with your hips knees and feet. Your right shoulder will be lower than your left.

You may prefer to form your hold first and then line up the bottom edge of the club face to your chosen site mark. If so your hold has to be carefully positioned on the club to bring the club face square to the target line at impact. For a straight shot, your shoulders remain parallel to the target line, along with your hips, knees and feet. Again, your right shoulder will be lower than your left.

When you practice, it is 'best practice' to check your alignment by placing a club across the front of your feet, parallel to your chosen target line. Pick up and hold another club across your shoulders, hips and knees, to check that each of these elements within your frame is parallel to the club on the ground. You can purchase alignment rods if you prefer.

HOLD OF THE CLUB (ALSO KNOWN AS THE GRIP)

Your left hand will provide the control and guidance for the golf shot. You can achieve a more secure hold on the club by wearing a golf glove on this hand. To position your left hand on the golf club adopt your normal swing plane posture and allow your arms to hang down naturally.

Allow the club to sit on the ground behind the golf ball, aligned to your target, in the position that it was made to sit. The club shaft and grip will be pointing up around the middle of your left thigh. This will encourage a good initial arm to shaft position, which will in turn enable your hands to quite naturally lead the club face into and through the impact area, naturally creating greater power and control.

You can formulate your hold on the golf club with your left hand first, followed by your right hand, or visa-versa. Try both ways and see which way you prefer. It is important however that your shoulders remain parallel to your chosen target line. The following description relates to a left hand first routine.

Hold the top of the grip of the golf club with the thumb and forefinger of your right hand. Offer your left hand to the grip of the golf club, with the back of your hand facing towards the target and the palm of your hand square to the face of the club head (the bottom edge of the club when using an Iron).

The club runs diagonally across your left hand and

will run from the base of your forefinger to just above the small fleshy area at the base of your little finger that forms when you bend your fingers. Allow your fingers to wrap around the grip of the golf club and you will see that the first joint of your forefinger will be directly under the grip. The fleshy pad, under your thumb at the heel of your hand, will be on top of the grip of the golf club slightly to the left. In fact it will be possible for you to hold the golf club with your left arm out in front of you horizontally and balance it across the first joint of your forefinger only, with the top end of the grip of the golf club under the small fleshy area at the base of your little finger, and your last three fingers entirely off the club!

Your hold of the golf club with your left hand will feel low down in your palm, which is important. Your thumb will be naturally pressing comfortably down on top of the clubs grip just right of centre, by degrees, to suit you. If your hold on the golf clubs grip with this hand is too high in the palm, more towards the centre of your wrist, this will not allow your wrist to hinge correctly and smoothly during the swing.

The tip of the thumb of your left hand will roughly be in line with the first joint of your forefinger, not elongated down the grip, which can restrict optimum flexibility of the left wrist. You feel the left side of your thumb up to around its middle joint, firmly, yet comfortably snuggled against the underside edge of the base of your forefinger. This support for your thumb will give your hold added stability and control at the top of your back swing.

As your left hand fingers wrap quite naturally around the grip of the golf club you will feel your last three fingers close together taking a firm hold. You understand that if this hold were to be too tight, then you would restrict the smooth natural action of your wrists during your swing.

The 'V' naturally formed by your left thumb and forefinger will naturally be aimed at a point around the centre of your right shoulder. When you look down on your completed left hand hold on the grip of the golf club, you will be able to see around two and a half knuckles from your overhead viewpoint.

Your right hand, when placed on the grip of the golf club correctly, will allow the club to be held securely. Your right wrist however will be allowed to hinge freely. This allows the club head to naturally swing and accelerate through the golf ball at speed. You will attain more consistency, control and distance from your shots by having a hold on the golf club

25

that is more technically correct and held firmly and sensitively.

Still adopting your natural swing plane posture with your left hand nicely in position on the golf clubs grip, allow your right arm to hang down naturally. Offer your right hand to the grip of your club with the palm of the hand square to the target line. For a straight shot, take the utmost care to keep your shoulders parallel to the target line.

Your right shoulder will be lower than your left. As your right hand moves into position feeling purposeful, yet light and relaxed, you align your palm with the clubface (the leading edge of an iron club). The grip of the golf club will run along the roots of your right hands fingers.

The second and third fingers of your right hand will be quite naturally close together, wrapping around and holding the grip of the club firmly but crucially allowing your wrists to hinge freely. Your third finger fits snugly against the forefinger of your left hand when assembling the overlapping or interlocking hold. There is more information on the types of hold, and the use of your little finger, coming up in this section.

The fleshy pad at the base of your right thumb will fit comfortably over, and press down comfortably on your left thumb concealing it. The life line on the palm of your right hand will run down along the top of your left thumb.

The forefinger of your right hand will be slightly triggered around the golf club with its tip lightly touching your right thumb. Your right thumb will be on top of the grip of your golf club, pointing down to the left. Your forefinger and thumb, once in position, will help you to gain a good feel down through the golf club to its centre of gravity and the club head.

With practice your hands will feel together with neither one dominating the other. The main pressure points will be felt on the second, third and little fingers of your left hand, the second and third fingers of your right hand in respect of the interlocking hold, and in addition, feeling more of your right forefinger in respect of the overlapping hold. These, together with the comfortable downward press onto your left thumb by the fleshy pad at the base of your right hand described earlier, make up the main sensitive, yet firm pressure points on the grip of the golf club. It is important that the hands work cooperatively together as a unit in a firm yet sensitive way.

The overlapping hold of the golf club (commonly known as the VARDON Grip), is where the little finger of your right hand comes off the golf club and wraps around the index finger of your left hand.

The interlocking hold of the golf club, is where the little finger of your right hand is off the golf club, and links with the index finger of your left hand which comes through to fit snuggly on top of your right hand between your third and little finger.

The two handed hold of the golf club, is where your hands just fit snuggly and comfortably side by side together around the grip of the club.

One of these holds will best suit your hands. The orthodox overlapping hold (known as the VARDON grip) is more widely used by professionals, giving a little more control in the left hand. The interlocking hold (or grip) can be beneficial to golfers with small hands and/or short fingers. The two handed hold (or grip), is sometimes preferred by golfers with weaker hands and wrists, and/or swings that have too much wrist action. This may result in a little reduction in the distance you attain from your shots, caused by this reduced wrist action, but giving you more control.

To realise your full potential you need a sound hold that is suitable and works for you, and it is important that your hands work together as a unit. This is an essential element, helping you to create a swing that is more natural, well - coordinated and powerful. The best advice is to have your grip checked by a competent Golf Professional.

As individuals we are all different anatomically, so it could be beneficial for you to change your hold to one that might be more suitable for you. You may also need to move your hold as a unit left or right very slightly by degrees to find the best position for you on the clubs grip, to enable you to bring the club face square to the target line at impact.

Turning your hold (grip) on the golf club as a unit, by degrees to the right, away from the target (known as a stronger position), will help to remove a tendency to slice the golf ball. Turning your hold on the golf club as a unit, by degrees to the left, towards the target (known as a weaker position), will help to remove a tendency to hook the golf ball. However do not use this as a substitute for poor posture and alignment.

During practice, experiment in small degrees to find the best hold position suitable for you. However, do check that your posture and alignment are correct (possibly with a friend), as you may be compensating for a faulty set up. This may feel unusual to start with, but experiment, be patient and persevere as you can benefit. You may consider having your grip and set up checked by a competent Golfing Professional to set you off on the right path going forward.

The golf club needs to be held firmly enough, but not throttled, so that it will stay in position in your hands during the swing. Your wrists however work best if they are able to hinge naturally during the swing, together with your forearms and shoulders free of any unnecessary tension.

At address hold the golf club with sensitivity and a firm lightness that maintains control. Your fingers will tend quite naturally to grip a little firmer during your swing anyway. To help you to condition and strengthen your hands, try holding a golf club in your chosen grip position while relaxing at home. This will help you to improve the condition and strength in your hands. Also using a mirror can help you check your chosen grip position and technique.

YOUR STANCE AND BALL POSITION

Place your left foot into position and then your right foot. Your toes, knees, hips, chest and more importantly your shoulders, are parallel to the target line you have chosen.

Ideally the width of your stance is just wide enough for you, to give you a stable and balanced basis for your swing. This should allow you to shift your weight and make a comfortable body turn. The width of your stance varies depending on the golf club you are using. The shorter the club the narrower your stance tends to be.

Women can have wider hips than men, and a lower centre of gravity. This can enhance weight shift and resistance during the swing action, so a wider stance, by degrees, can be beneficial.

As a guide, the insides of your feet are around shoulder width when playing your 5 Iron upwards. Your feet may be a touch wider when driving the golf ball. Your stance will reduce from there down through your short Irons. It will be at its narrowest (around the width of your hips) when using a wedge.

The width of your stance is achieved by the placement of your right leg away from your left. Given your own unique build, you will need to experiment to find the ideal stance solution for you and find the low point in your swing for the club you are employing.

Both of your feet feel comfortable and alive. Your left foot is turned around twenty degrees off square towards the target, depending on your individual preference. This helps you to transfer your weight during your swing and turn your chest more naturally towards the target, achieving a more balanced finish. Do not overdo this though as you can restrict the flexibility of your left leg which can restrict your natural leg movement.

You right foot can be set square to the target line (many golfers prefer this), or perhaps a few degrees or so angled off square back away from the target. This helps you to keep your weight on the inside of your right foot and leg during your backswing, which is important.

If you have less flexibility, set your left foot square to the target line, which will give your left leg more flexibility and help your turn. The capability to turn your hips to around thirty to forty degrees off square, back away from the target is ideal, depending on your flexibility. Working to improve your flexibility will also help you.

The golf club moves in a circular motion in your swing plane around your body. The lowest point is where the path of the club head passes around the centre of your chest, providing your set up is good. For the average golfer, the ideal position of the golf ball is the low point for the particular club that you are using. Where the golfer is more athletic and advanced, he or she may have developed a good strong leg action. If this is the case then the ball may be best positioned, by degrees, further forward in the stance to suit the player.

When playing your driver off the tee, the ball is positioned opposite the inside of the heel of your left foot, with some players preferring the ball, by degrees, further to the left. It is teed up with half of the ball above the top edge of the face of the driver, a touch lower if playing into the wind. Aim for the bottom of your swing arc to be a few inches behind the ball. This will encourage a level to upward sweep through the ball, imparting over spin and achieving a more powerful penetrating trajectory.

Through practice and experimentation with your driver and other woods (say a three wood, where the ball may be, by degrees, placed further back and teed lower), you can find the best placement and tee height suitable for you, for each club.

When playing your 5 Iron, the golf ball is played from a point between your left heel and the centre of your stance. When playing your 6 Iron down through to a wedge, the ball will be played further back towards the centre of your stance by degrees, with the wedge being played around the centre of your stance. Let your golf club sit how it was made to sit. Your stance narrows as you move down through your irons of course. On the tee the ball can of course be teed up, not too high though, just nicely off the ground to promote confidence where required by the individual.

Sound golfing fundamental technique (posture, hold, stance and alignment), will allow you to naturally hold the golf club in the position it was made to sit in. Your golf ball will naturally be in the ideal position in relation to the club that you are using, providing the clubface is square to your target line and you are set up correctly.

PRE-SHOT ALIGNMENT

Your toes are parallel to your chosen target line for a standard shot. Your knees are comfortably flexed above your feet and are also parallel to your chosen target line. Your hips too are parallel and your shoulders are positioned over your comfortably flexed knees.

WEIGHT DISTRIBUTION

When using your driver, with the golf ball teed up, your weight distribution is around ten percent in favour of your right side at address. That means only a slight transference of weight of around five percent from left to right. This will help to keep your upper body behind the ball, setting you up to encourage an ideal level to upwards sweep through the ball. By adopting a wider stance when using the driver, this naturally places your head more to the right side. That in itself moves your weight to the right side, creating a shallower more powerful swing arc into the back of the golf ball.

When using your utility woods, or long irons of a 5 iron or above, around a 50:50 balanced position is ideal. This together with the ideal ball position, around the bottom of the arc of your swing, will help you to sweep the golf ball away with little or no divot.

When playing a short iron (6 or 7 iron upwards) then your weight distribution is ideally around 60:40 in favour of your left side. This, together with a narrower stance and your head in a more central position, will help you to achieve a subtle downward swing through the golf ball naturally gaining more backspin, accuracy and control. The ideal angle of approach of the club head will result in a divot that is narrow and shallow. Remember when you are distributing your weight to 60:40, you are only shifting your weight by 10% to one side, so be careful not to overdo it.

Front to back your balance is best served with your weight in the area around the balls of your feet. Not rigidly set in stone but athletically with a light springiness. This will also promote great feel and tempo for the shot in hand.

GETTING READY

Your elbows come into and are brushing comfortably against your sides naturally pointing downwards to your hips.

Your posterior and the muscles and tendons of your lower back, naturally act as a steadying factor and counterbalance to your golf swing at address. This helps you to create the ideal balanced and athletic feeling, front to back, centred round the balls of your feet.

It is worth repeating here that front to back your balance is best served with your weight in the area around the balls of your feet. Not rigidly set in stone, but athletically with a light springiness that will also promote great feel and tempo.

Your thighs and knees are comfortably flexed

and slightly drawn together. You feel your weight slightly more on the insides of your legs, thighs and feet.

You feel steady and balanced ready for action with your weight comfortably around the balls of your feet. You get the feeling of being secure upon but not rooted to the ground beneath your feet. You trust that your foot action will occur naturally during your swing. Your legs feel comfortable, alive and ready for action.

Your right leg feels comfortably braced, and is in a flexed position. Your right leg stays steadily and comfortably in this position during your backswing. Your left leg and knee feel flexible, which assists your hips to turn, helping you to make a sound smooth swing, in plane, back and through the ball.

THE WAGGLE

Whether or not to incorporate the waggle into your routine is a personal choice. With club in hand, you are simply gaining a feel for the club, and that helps you achieve a smooth transition from address to the start of your backswing. Try and find the clubs balance point (its centre of gravity) as you waggle, as this can enhance your overall feeling of the club head. Also you can gain valuable feedback that your hands are working together as a unit and able to produce the required smooth wrist action.

You hold the golf club sensitively yet firmly enough to keep the club in position within your grip throughout your swing. Your wrists, arms and shoulders feel supple and fluid, they are free of any unnecessary tension as you waggle the golf club. You sense and feel the centre of gravity of the club in your hands. This can assist your arms to swing with fluidity and a good tempo.

Your waggle can best serve you by being controlled and smooth, and can be a rehearsal of the initial part of your swing. This can help to promote a considered, controlled and smooth takeaway at the start of your swing.

Two or three waggles will normally be sufficient, however do whatever works best for you, your style and personality. However keep the same routine on every full shot, to promote consistency.

THE TRIGGER

This is an initial action that you can incorporate into your routine to help you to initiate your swing smoothly. Examples of this could be a deliberate blink of the eyes, turning (not lifting) your chin slightly to the right, consciously and comfortably breathing out, or a subtle slight clenching of the toes. Alternatively this might be a gentle pressure and release of your thumbs on the golf club or a very slight forward press of the hands. Find whatever works best for you to promote a smooth takeaway of the club.

THE TAKE AWAY

As you steadily take a breath, hold the base of your neck and your spine comfortably steady. You focus your attention on the back of the golf ball. Your hold on the golf club is 'sensitively firm' in cooperation with your wrists, arms and shoulders that feel comfortably fluid.

As you steadily breathe out, you make a subtle steady downward, anti-clockwise movement of your left shoulder within your swing plane.

Your left shoulder continues to move down and to the right within your swing plane towards its eventual destination under your chin. You can feel the inside of your upper left arm close to the left side of your torso.

In coordination with your shoulders the golf club moves comfortably and steadily back with your left arm steadily rotating clockwise. Your wrists do not break during the takeaway process.

As you start back you maintain the V formed from your wrists to your elbows at address. Also you maintain the natural angle created by the back of your left hand and forearm at address, all the way through the backswing, in order to keep the club face square to the swing line.

Your left arm continues to rotate clockwise and stretches naturally and is reasonably straight and comfortable. Let it be a natural movement (your arm does not have to be dead straight). Play within your physical capabilities.

THE BACK SWING

Remember, the main objective of creating a good backswing, is to provide the optimum position from which to swing the golf club down and through the ball.

As the club head fans away and upwards on your swing plane, your right arm pulls back and folds naturally at the right time.

Your wrists break naturally, and reach the desired fully cocked set position, by the time your hands reach waist height (around level with your belly button). At this point the palm of your right hand is facing forward at a right angle to your swing plane. Your club will be held vertically in plane, and feel nicely balanced within your hold. This is also a good check point to ensure that you are swinging in plane, and not too flat. Alternatively, you may prefer to consciously set the wrist cock, after the takeaway of course, earlier on in your back swing, if that suits you better. However, avoid twisting the club off the square address position.

Your hips rotate clockwise from left to the right to around thirty to forty degrees from your target line depending on your level of flexibility. They do not employ any swaying action laterally from left to right. This is very important.

Be careful not to over swing your golf club, maintaining control is more important. The length of your back swing will to some extent depend also upon your particular build and flexibility. Setting your right foot pointing straight ahead at a right angle to your chosen target line, will afford more control to the golfer who has a tendency to over swing.

You feel the effect of the back swing quite naturally on the inside of your right foot and on the inside of your, comfortably braced, right thigh and around your stomach. This resistance felt in your right thigh and your stomach provides the necessary resistance in the backswing that converts into power down and through the ball. This also avoids the hips overturning.

Around half way back you feel the effect of the swing on the ball of your left foot below your big toe. Your left knee is pulled by the action of your hips, so that it points to a position around the back of your golf ball. This happens quite naturally.

Your swing is naturally at its longest when employing the driver, and shortens down through the irons, to be at its shortest when using a wedge.

Your hold on the golf club is maintained at the conclusion (the top of) your backswing, to loosen is to lose control.

Your left shoulder brushes under your chin on a full shot thus confirming a full shoulder turn. Your left side feels comfortable and you feel the effect of your swing on the left side of your back as your swing reaches the top of the backswing.

Your balance is maintained and your fulcrum (the base of your neck) remains steady. At the top of your backswing the golf club, will be in the ideal position for your swing plane, pointing over the edge of your right shoulder towards your chosen target. It's worth repeating here, that at the top of your back swing you will predominantly feel the effect of your swing on the inside of your right thigh, on the inside of your right foot and in the area of your stomach. You will also feel the swing on the left side of your back and on ball of your left foot just below your left big toe. You will also feel the pull of your folded right arm, against the natural stretch of your left arm. By letting your right arm work naturally, with no conscious effort to keep the inside of your upper right arm rigidly by your right side, you can avoid, unnecessarily, restricting the width of your swing arc.

At the top of your backswing, if the back of your left hand is in line with your forearm, this will bring the club face square through the ball. This is providing that your arms swing in coordination with your body rotation, in line with your swing plane. If the left wrist is bowed, then the club face will travel through the ball with the clubface closed, unless some compensating body, arm or wrist action takes place. If the left wrist is cupped, then the clubface will travel through the ball with the clubface open, unless again some compensating body, arm or wrist action takes place.

COMMENCEMENT OF THE DOWNSWING

Your eyes are focused on the back of your golf ball precisely on the spot where the club head meets the ball. Initially your head and shoulders remain in the 'top of your backswing' position. It is important to make these initial downswing moves steadily. This can help you to achieve optimal timing, by coordinating the turn of your body to allow your arms to swing down.

At the optimal time, the angles created in your wrists are naturally released, to create and apply the power created through the golf ball.

At the start of your downswing, it is important that your weight remains on your right foot, resist any temptation to throw your legs early towards the target. You purposely move your knees steadily and laterally to the left. Your hips naturally follow by reacting and turning proportionately and steadily anti-clockwise. Your swing is led by your left side pulling steadily anti-clockwise within your swing plane, and you feel this. However, at this early point, your right side is subordinate and relaxed and has, to some extent, not yet reacted to the commencement of the downswing. Because of this early action of your knees, you will feel at this stage a controlled shift of the weight from the ball of your left toe and the inside of your right leg to a fairly balanced position between both legs. You will also feel a natural tension in your left side created by the aforementioned action.

THE DOWNSWING

Because of the initial pulling action of your left side, your left shoulder is naturally pulled, anticlockwise, down and back within your swing plane. You feel your torso turning into your left arm helping to keep your swing in plane. Also, the inside of your upper right arm comfortably moves to meet your right side. Your head remains steady.

Your arms, wrists and hands rotate down steadily anticlockwise on their swing path, and around half way down your reasonably straight left arm is approximately parallel to the ground. The club feels balanced in your hands and is pointing naturally to the sky above. You feel the effect of the downswing on the inside of your left thigh and foot. At the same time the effect of the downswing has moved the feeling on the inside of your right thigh down more towards your right knee and the inside of your right foot. As your hands approach your right thigh the club shaft is approximately parallel to the ground. Your hands then release into and through the ball and the shaft of the club is in line with your left forearm. Around the same time, your right knee and foot push laterally parallel to the target line contributing added momentum. The feeling you experience is felt more on the inside of the ball of your right foot below your big toe. The inside of your left leg feels comfortably braced to accept your swing into and through the ball.

Your wrists un-cock naturally as your swing builds up pace coming down and through the ball, providing there is a feeling of fluidity in the area of your forearms and wrists. The V formed by your wrists to your elbows at address is virtually duplicated as the club head swings through the ball. Your left arm continues its pull, and you can power through with your right shoulder followed by your right knee and arm. Your right wrist and hand release into and through the ball. You time this release perfectly, in perfect combination with your turn and the feeling of the inside of your right leg and foot pushing through to the left, parallel to the target line.

You feel that your swing has rhythm (flow) and your own natural tempo (swing speed). Your swing also has controlled power, steadily building up thus creating the utmost timing into and through the ball.

THE FOLLOW THROUGH

Your right shoulder moves past your chin and continues to rotate naturally anticlockwise from its low point, as your swing naturally follows your swing plane to the left of your target line.

Your right arm rolls over your left arm and straightens out towards the target along with your straight left arm. The back of your right hand, when around waist height, is facing away from you in your swing plane. Whereas on the backswing, the back of your right hand, at waist height, was facing behind you in your swing plane. This shows the importance of allowing your wrists to take their natural course during the swing.

You continue to feel the effect of your swing on the inside of your left thigh and foot. As your hands reach around waist height you will continue to feel the effect of the swing on the inside of your left thigh and also on the outside of your left foot. Your knees naturally come together. You feel your upper right arm swing across your chest. Your left arm naturally folds followed by your right with your upper left arm comfortably positioned to your left side.

THE POISED BALANCED FINISH

You still feel the effect of your swing on the inside of your left thigh and on the outside of your left foot. Your knees are comfortably together with your right foot on its toes. The natural tilt of your body will be from left to right, and the shaft of your golf club is behind your neck. You achieve a comfortable, relaxed and balanced finish with the front of your upper body facing, by degrees, left of the target. The golf club is held comfortably high over your left shoulder and the club shaft is behind the back of your neck. You hold your poised balanced position, and observe the shot you have created. What does the flight of the ball tell you and what can you learn? (It is a good idea to build this into your practice sessions too).

LEARNING TO CURVE YOUR GOLF BALL LEFT TO RIGHT

Before learning how to do this, it is important that you have developed the ability to play the straight shot. To do this, you will have developed good posture and alignment. You will also hold the club correctly for you, in order to bring the face of the club head square and solidly into the back of the golf ball. Even after achieving this you may find that you have a natural tendency to play the ball with a fade. If this turns out to be the case, then you can build this into your game strategy, knowing that your game will hold up better under pressure.

You can learn to curve the golf ball from left to right by differing degrees, from a slight fade, through to much more of a curved ball depending on the strategic circumstances of the shot in hand. The further to the left you align yourself, the more pronounced the curve on the golf ball will be. When playing this shot off the tee, tee the ball lower. You may find that setting up more to the right side gives you more confidence. This can open up the target area, however be specific with your target point.

Remember also, that the golf ball will not travel as far with a fade as your normal straight shot, unless the lie of the land favours that type of shot, so you will have to factor this into your thinking by using a longer club.

Remember too that it is important to have the clubface set up square to your target line, as you would when executing a straight shot. In order to produce the curved trajectory from left to right that you require, simply adjust the alignment of your body, including your feet, knees, hips and shoulders, by degrees, to the left of your target. Place your hold on the club, keeping the club face square to the target line. At impact the clubface will be open to the line of your swing, thus imparting clockwise sidespin upon your golf ball. The ball starts out left in line with the alignment of your body, and then curves to the right back towards your target. The further left that you position and align yourself, the more pronounced will be the curve on the shot.

With sound practice and work you can develop your skills in this more advanced area of the game. You will gain experience and an understanding of just how far left you have to position yourself, to create the desired amount of curve that you require for a particular situation. More advanced players can learn to shape shots, to a certain degree, by using their wrists and hands, without any material change to their set up and alignment.

For right handers, when playing your fade shot, the following will help you to prevent yourself from hitting the golf ball straight left. Purposely feel a little more pressure in your left hand and a little less in your right hand. This encourages your right hand to release slightly later, thus avoiding your right hand dominating the shot and closing the clubface at impact. Feel how you want your hands and forearms to work the ball. The more you want to curve the shot left to right, the more subtle pressure is felt in favour of your left hand. Lead with your left hand. Also during the follow through the elbow of your left arm will be further away from your

CHRISTOPHER PEAKE

left side. Do not overdo these additional measures though, practice by degrees and find your own way. You will find this very rewarding and fulfilling, opening up a whole new way to play your golf.

For left handers, when playing your draw shot, the following will help you to prevent yourself from hitting the golf ball straight left. Purposely feel a little more pressure in your right hand and a little less in your left. This will help to avoid your left hand dominating the shot and seeking to open the clubface, thus counteracting the required left to right spin upon your golf ball. The more you wish to curve the golf ball left to right, then the more subtle pressure is felt in favour of your right hand. Do not overdo these additional measures, practice by degrees and find your own way. You will find this experience very rewarding and fulfilling, opening up new possibilities in your game.

Another factor to understand is that, if your golf ball is on a tight lie, there is more of a natural tendency to impart fade onto the shot. This is because you will quite naturally lead more with your left hand (right hand for a left hander) to get the ball airborne, imparting left to right sidespin onto your golf ball (right to left sidespin for a left hander). Also this type of shot is not possible with your short irons where the natural backspin imparted to your golf ball tends to override the sidespin factor.

LEARNING TO CURVE YOUR GOLF BALL RIGHT TO LEFT

Again, before learning how to do this you have to be able to hit the golf ball straight having good posture, good alignment and the ability to hold your golf club correctly for you. This is in order to bring the face of the golf club square and solidly into the back of the ball. Even after achieving this, you may find that you have a natural tendency to draw the ball. Again, if this turns out to be the case, then you can build this into your game strategy, knowing that your game will hold up better under pressure.

You can learn to curve your golf ball from right to left by differing degrees from a slight draw, to a more pronounced curve of the ball depending upon the strategic circumstances of the shot in hand.

The further to the right you and align yourself, the more pronounced the curve upon the golf ball will be. When playing off the tee, tee the ball up higher. You may find that setting up on the left side, opens up the landing area and gives you added confidence. However, be precise with your target point.

Also remember that if you are a right hander playing a draw shot, the golf ball will travel further than your normal straight shot, so you will have to factor this in by using a shorter club.

However if you are a left hander playing a fade shot then the golf ball will travel a shorter distance than your normal straight shot, so you will have to factor this in by using a longer club.

An important thing to remember is to have the clubface set up square to your target line, as you would when executing a straight shot. In order to produce the curved trajectory from right to left that you require, simply adjust the alignment of your body, including your feet, hips and shoulders, by degrees to the right of your target. Place your hold on the club, keeping the club face square to the target line. At impact, the clubface will be closed to the line of your swing, imparting anti-clockwise sidespin upon your golf ball. The ball starts out to the right in line with the alignment of your body, before curving around left to your target. With sound practice and experience you can develop your skills further. You will learn to judge how far to the right you have to position yourself, to create the amount of curve for any given situation. More advanced players can learn to shape shots to a certain extent, using their wrists and hands, without any material difference to their set up and alignment.

In the case of a right hander playing a draw shot, to help you to prevent yourself from hitting your golf ball straight right, purposely feel a little more pressure in your right hand and a little less in your left. This helps to avoid your left hand from dominating the shot, and seeking to open the clubface, thus counteracting the required right to left spin upon your golf ball. The more that you wish to curve the golf ball right to left, the more subtle pressure is felt in favour of your right hand. You will feel your right arm and hand roll, by degrees, through the ball.

Again do not overdo these additional measures, practice by degrees and find your own way. As was said earlier in the text you will find this experience very rewarding and fulfilling, opening up a whole new way for you to play your golf.

In the case of a left hander playing a fade shot, the following will help you to prevent yourself from hitting your golf ball straight right. Purposely feel a little more pressure in your right hand and a little less in your left hand, thus avoiding your left hand dominating the shot and closing the clubface at impact. The more you wish to curve the golf ball right to left, the more subtle pressure is felt in favour of your right hand. Lead with your right hand. Do not overdo this though, practice by degrees and find your own way. You will find this very rewarding and fulfilling, opening up a whole new way to play your golf.

For a right hander another factor to be aware of is, that if your golf ball is teed up high or sitting up in the grass, then this leads to a tendency for a shot to move from right to left (left to right for a left hander). This is because your hands are more free and able to swing the golf club though the ball.

SOME OTHER THOUGHTS

When practising, either on the practice area or the driving range, it can be useful to go with a friend and video your respective swing actions. This can be very beneficial to the individual to actually see themselves moving within the swing rather than how they imagine they move. This can be very enlightening for the individual and help them to move forward with and develop their game further.

When you arrive at the golf course, by all means have a warm up, a few stretches, a few practice swings and spend a little time on the putting green. This is a time for you to tune into your golfing persona, be determined to concentrate well when assessing and playing your shots, and switching off to enjoy the time in between. You warm up, gently stretching your muscles and tune into your personal tempo and rhythm. Your intention is to play within yourself, to be in the moment and be patient, and give the course the best you can with the best that you have this day.

You accept now, that by the very nature of the game, there will be challenges ahead. However, you can walk off each of the eighteen holes knowing that you tried your best, which can only be a good thing for your wellbeing. Enjoy the golf course and its environment, how lucky you are!

Wherever possible, have a plan of action to play the course, and go over in your mind your pre-shot routines. There may be a particular aspect of your game that you want to use as a 'positive pre-swing thought, for instance, 'make solid contact with the ball'. All these things can be beneficial to your game. Be fair and kind to yourself and determine to enjoy the day.

After your round, remember where you strategized and played well, think about what could have turned out better and what you can do to improve things. Then head off to the practice area at the next opportunity to make improvements to you game and enjoy the process. Who knows what you can achieve. Good golfing!

THE SHORT GAME

Introduction

The short game is an important element of the game of golf, as is the full swing and a sound strategy. It is important therefore, if you are to make steady progress, that you are practicing the right techniques for you. For example in the way you stand and align yourself and the way in which you hold the golf club. With this in mind it is well worth having a few lessons with a Golf Professional to set you off on the right path.

You can then, with commitment, patience and practice, make steady and sure progress. It is hoped that the information in this section will help the many of you that play golf to reach your full potential on your golfing journey.

The suggestions here require you to carefully and decisively think and apply measures to improve. Thus helping you, 'by degrees', to achieve positive game improvements. This is important and is mentioned often in the narrative. A small yet significant change can often be beneficial to you, in your quest for steady improvement.

As we have said, a small subtle change can lead to a game improvement; however avoid making too many changes too soon. Adopt changes steadily to help you to improve where you feel necessary.

Strive to do the best that you can on each of the shots that you are faced with. Going out onto the golf course in this frame of mind, will help you keep a balanced more philosophical viewpoint about the various challenges and outcomes of the day. You will also be more relaxed and happy.

You can develop sound reliable routines and thought processes, enabling you to 'just play the game' and enhance your creativity, enjoyment and fulfilment.

PUTTING

Putting is an individual matter for the golfer, with many different styles, all with the careful 'aim' of getting the golf ball into the hole.

It is well worth spending some of your time researching and learning about this area of the game, in particular your stance, posture and hold on the putter.

Up to half of your shots in a round of golf are on the putting surface. With this in mind, it is well worth your time to invest in a putting lesson with your local Golf Professional.

You can develop sound and effective techniques and pre-shot routines that you can trust. This will then free you up to:

'FEEL, AND PLAY YOUR SHOT'S IN THE MOMENT, THUS ACHIEVE MORE SUCCESS IN GETTING THE GOLF BALL INTO THE HOLE'.

Your eyes can have a more accurate view of the putt in hand, when they are directly over the ball, on your chosen target line, or slightly inside the target line.

The palm of your left hand is parallel with the face of your putter. Your left hand can be above your right hand on the putter, or below your right hand.

When putting, your left hand hold of the putter is more in the palm, with the wrist held up slightly. This helps to prevent the left wrist from hinging and rolling to the left, thus moving the face of your putter to the left of the target as it moves through the ball. This also gives you assurance and confidence in your left hand hold in terms of the direction of the putt. Your left thumb is on top of the grip pointing slightly to the right. Your left forefinger can be used as a steadying influence, where the right hand is placed below the left, if deployed over the right hand fingers or on the putter shaft as the putter moves back from the ball.

The fingers and finger tips of your right hand can provide you with the necessary feel for the pace of the putt, where the right hand is below the left. However, where the right hand is placed above the left you will not have as much of that feel in the right hand, relying more on the rocking of your shoulders to provide the ideal pace on the putt.

Where the right hand is below the left, the right hand thumb can be placed on top of the grip, pointing down and slightly to the left, with the pad below the thumb partially covering your left thumb. The right hand fingers are wrapped lightly underneath the grip. The right forefinger can be separated and touch the thumb (triggered), to create added feel for the putt. Also, if preferred, your left forefinger can rest on top the last three fingers of your right hand.

Alternatively, again where the right hand is below the left, your right thumb can be under the grip with the fingers on top in various positions with various pressure points ensuing. It is best to align the putter face initially with your right hand with the palm square to the face of your putter and your chosen target line. Then, keeping your same posture and your shoulders parallel to the target line, apply your left hand to the grip with the palm square to the putter head and target line. You then release your right hand and re –apply it, with your thumb under the grip and your fingers on top, in whatever configuration you choose. Experiment and find a style that feels comfortable and works for you.

Focus on the hole and the ball, not the putter head, as you make your putting stroke.

For short length putts, as the ball starts on its way, you can try to 'just listen' for the ball to drop into the hole, 'no looking - just listen'. For longer putts just wait a moment until the golf ball moves out of your sight. This technique can also be used as a measure, in practice and during play, to help a golfer to overcome a tendency to move his or her head, during the putting stroke.

Your shoulders, chest, elbows, knees and toes are ideally parallel to the target line. However, if you prefer a slightly open stance, you can keep your shoulders and elbows square to the target line, along with the face of your putter, perhaps with a slightly firmer hold with your right hand. Alternatively, you can set your body alignment in line with your open stance, opening the face of your putter, so that it is in line with your chosen target. However this will exert a certain amount of left to right spin on the ball. This can be an inconsistent method, although keeping your right elbow comfortably close to your right side, and adopting a slightly firmer hold with your right hand can help. Plus of course, adopting the square to target left hand palm position, and practice of course.

Your right elbow is ideally tucked comfortably into your side close to your right hip.

A confident, relaxed and assertive state of mind will assist you on the green. Remember a successful putt you have made in the past and then focus on the putt in hand – picture yourself being successful now.

Ideally there cannot be any forward, backward or sideways movement of your body frame during the putting stroke. You may like to try bringing your knees comfortably together slightly to give you more stability.

Your head needs to remain still and steady during the putting stroke and is a major factor in a successful putting technique.

You feel that your feet are comfortable on the putting surface (gently waggling your toes can help). This can help you to feel nice and comfortable over the ball. Concentrate on making a smooth putting stroke.

During your pre-shot routine, you breathe comfortably in through your nose and out through your mouth. Smile, relax and gently breathe out before commencing your putting stroke. Be decisive and enjoy the process.

Treat every putt as a straight putt (towards your chosen target).

Where there is a borrow in the ground, either left or right, aim the putter at your chosen target mark which could be a blade of grass, or an indentation in the ground. Visualise the shot and focus on stroking the ball towards the hole, having previously lined up your putter with your chosen target mark. The slope of the green will help to guide your ball along the route you have chosen, towards the hole. On fast greens, the ball will break more than on a slower surface. Bear in mind also, that the roll and direction on the ball can be affected in windy conditions, so take account of this.

Ensure that the lie of your putter and length of shaft are suitable for you. To help you promote consistency, it is preferable that the sole of your putter sits level on level ground without the heel or the toe unnaturally raised- up. Let the putter sit where it was made to sit. This enables the putter to perform well when used with good technique, care and precision.

Your wrists are comfortably held up, by degrees, to assist keeping the putter head on line. This naturally helps to keep the wrists more passive and in a good position during the putting stroke. This also improves consistency on the greens.

Your hold on the putter is lightly firm, perhaps a little firmer with your left hand for a straight forward putt, keeping both forearms relaxed. Control with feel is what you are looking to achieve.

You maintain the angle created by the back of your left hand and your left forearm from the start to the finish of the shot.

Take care to ensure that the putter face is precisely set up to stroke the ball along the target line. Every putter has a sweet spot and it is the sweet spot that needs to meet the golf ball during the stroke, thus promoting increased feel, confidence and consistency.

You may like to try the following in practice sessions: Hover your putter slightly above the ground just before commencement of your putting stroke. However it is important to keep the putter face square to the target line. Hovering can help to ensure a smooth start as part of your developed and trusted putting routine. This can also be used as a temporary measure to help a golfer remedy a tendency to snatch at a putt on the takeaway. If you have a steady hand, and you feel confident, you may like to give it a try out on the course.

The take away of your putter is ideally smooth and steadily controlled. The tempo of your putting swing reflects your style and personality (the way you go about things); just the same as with all other shots you play on the course. Be yourself, and let your personality and individuality shine through in your game. Good tempo that suits you (your own pace), is very helpful towards achieving a good putting technique.

Develop your tried and trusted pre-shot routines through patient and thoughtful practice. Take these with you to the course, trusting and sticking with them for your round that day.

Always mark, lift and clean your ball when on the green. Please take responsibility to repair any pitch mark that your golf ball has made to the putting surface. Pitch repairers are cheap to buy and are an essential, must have, item to carry with you. This helps to maintain the condition of the greens on the golf course. You will no doubt agree that all golfers benefit from that! It also helps and motivates the green keeping staff, who will feel that their work is appreciated. With players working in partnership with the green keeping staff, it becomes much easier to keep the greens to a good standard. Great putting surfaces make for great golf!

To help with the alignment of your golf ball to your chosen target line, when replacing your ball marker with your golf ball, you can align the printed trademark to your chosen target line.

An arm and shoulder putting stroke is often more

consistent, combined with a fairly narrow stance that feels comfortable to you. However a wider stance, by degrees, may suit your style, providing you feel comfortable and retain a feel for the shot.

Putting is a very individual matter with more wrist action sometimes being preferred by the individual golfer and/or a wider stance adopted. However it is important that you feel comfortable over the ball, and that the putter face is precisely aligned to your chosen target line. It is also important to ensure that the angle created by the back of your left hand and forearm at address is replicated into the ball. Learning to do this with a reasonable amount of consistently is a challenge, and can be achieved with practice.

The correct assessment of the length and run of a putt (the feel of the putt) is essential .If you were to roll the ball towards the target with your hand, you would probably get it quite close, so by just imagining the putter as an extension of your arm, can improve your judgement of pace.

Having made your assessment of the feel and pace of the putt, you must always smoothly and steadily accelerate (at the desired tempo), the putting stroke through the ball. Know your natural tempo and stick with that for best results.

A short putt requires a short backswing and a short follow through, preferably of the same length like a pendulum. Over swinging is best avoided.

The position of your golf ball should preferably be at a point, by degrees, between the centre of your comfortable stance and your left foot. Not too far forward however, so as to compromise and overstretch your natural putting action. This encourages a slightly upward contact through the ball, helping it to set off on a good roll towards its destination. You keep your weight distribution comfortably by degrees more towards your left side as this helps to keep your head steady. When looking at the target line when you are over the ball, you can if you wish swivel, not lift, your head. Also let your putter sit where it was made to sit, as this will help you to get the dynamics right here. You can widen your stance, by degrees, in windy conditions to aid your balance and stability.

During the very early part of your putting stroke, your putter can be taken straight back away from the golf ball. This should be a natural manoeuvre for you and not forced, and without turning the left hand palm off its square position on the grip of the putter. Depending on the length of backward motion, the putter head will naturally move slightly, by degrees, inside the target line. During practice, or actual play, you should ensure that the putter head is not allowed to move outside of the target line.

When practising take up your putting stance over the ball. Then try holding the top of the grip of your putter against the bridge of your nose, directly between your eyes, with your thumb and forefinger. Allow the putter head to drop straight down with its centre behind the ball to check that your eyes are directly over the target line. Also get a colleague or friend to check you in this respect during practice.

LONG PUTTING

During long putting practice, find a fairly flat portion of the putting green. Hold a golf ball in your hand and roll it with your hand towards the target, helping you to get a feel for the distance of the putt. Then stroke another ball with your putter towards the target, using your developed and trusted putting routine.

Work towards your forearms and wrists being comfortably relaxed, and the inside of your upper arms comfortably close to your sides. Your arms then work in cooperation with the 'mini turn' of your chest.

Your hold on the putter is light, yet firm, find that balance that works for you. This helps you to feel comfortable and sense just what is required to play the shot well.

The ability to measure distance through developing a 'feel' for the distance of a putt is your goal. You are able to do this by judging the length of 'mini swing' you require and applying your personal rhythm, and tempo, to create the ideal momentum through the golf ball. This is crucial to achieving consistency, and reducing the number of putting strokes you take on the greens.

When long putting during actual play mark, lift and clean your golf ball and repair your pitch mark. Then with your golf ball in hand visualise and feel the shot. This will help you gain a feel for the distance of the putt. Apply that feel to the shot, using your putter as an extension of your hands.

When assessing a long putt, pick a target mark to align your putter with. This may be the hole or a point between your balls current position and the hole.

When faced with a long putt, pick a site mark around a yard in front of your ball on your chosen target line. This could be a blade of grass for instance. Line up the face of your putter precisely square to your chosen site mark. This can help you to stroke your golf ball along your chosen target line more successfully.

When on the green, you pay attention to your playing partners as they play their putts. You can obtain valuable feedback on the prevailing conditions, contours and speed of the putting surface.

Your 'aim' is to develop your own trusted putting routine that you can take with you to the golf course, thus improving your consistency and confidence. This then 'frees you up' to just play the shot and focus on getting your golf ball into the hole.

READING THE GREEN

Putting plays a large part in the game of golf and requires good concentration, which starts as you approach the greens arena and setting. So switch yourself on, make your assessments and take sound decisive decisions. Challenge yourself to subsequently leave the green having given your best regardless of the outcome. If you do this you will maintain a good feeling about this aspect of your game and relish each situation you are presented with. You will enjoy the game more and more, and by maintaining a good frame of mind, you will become more consistent and successful.

You can work on, and develop, routines that are tailor made for you and that you can rely upon. It is hoped that this section will help you to achieve this.

The first thing to remember is that only a tiny part of the surface area of your golf ball is in touch with the putting surface at any given moment in time. So it pays dividends to look carefully at the route it will take towards the hole. You will understand that any surface impediment, however slight, can alter its course.

NOTE- BY APPLYING YOUR CONCENTRATION TO A CONSIDERED AND DECISIVE APPROACH TO PUTTING, YOU WILL SAVE TIME IN THE LONG RUN BY HAVING FEWER PUTTS TO MAKE.

When playing a particular hole on the golf course, you can observe other greens in view. Look and see the contours, pin positions and any hazards and bunkers. This can assist your strategy later in your round.

As you approach the green, observe its contours, slopes and general appearance. Look for high and low points in the layout of the green, and make your way to the low side. Is the green in an open setting, which may result in dryer and therefore faster prevailing surface conditions? Alternatively if the green is in a more sheltered position, it could be retaining more moisture. This could result in a slower putting surface.

Look at the green from the low side, to gain a picture of the overall contours that could influence your putting strategy.

As you walk onto the putting surface, try to get a feel for the texture of the grass beneath your feet. Always repair the pitch mark that you have made with your golf ball. This helps to keep the green in tip top condition and gives players the best opportunity to score well.

Feel and assess the strength and direction of any prevailing breeze. You may decide to take account of these factors, which could have an effect upon your putt when assessing the line later.

After marking, cleaning and replacing your golf ball on the putting surface, look at the putt from the low side. Assess whether the putt is on an upslope or down slope and gain a feel for the overall distance.

Also observe the cut of the green between your golf ball and the target. Assess whether the grain is with or against the roll of the putt, or from side to side, or possibly a combination of these conditions. If there are darker areas of the green between the ball and the target then the grain is likely to be against you, whereas if the grass is more light and shiny then the grain will probably be with you. These conditions will most likely have an effect on the speed and direction of your golf ball.

You may like to view the putt from behind the hole, sit on your haunches, or bend down if you can. Assess the possible effect on the rotation of the golf ball as it approaches the hole and slows down during the last quarter of the putt.

Look for anything around the hole that may change the path of the putt from its intended line. Assess which side of the hole is higher and the point at which the golf ball will enter the hole.

Before playing the putt, crouch or bend down if you can and look at the putt from around two metres behind the golf ball. Utilising the information you have gathered, you will have gained a good feel for the pace and line of the putt.

On occasions where the break of your putt is not clear cut, then you can adopt the plumb bob technique. This is where you hold your putter up in front of you. Grip it with your thumb and forefinger. Let your putter hang down vertically in front of your dominant eye (closing your other eye of course). The shaft is set to the centre of the hole. Try it and see.

It is important to develop a considered, yet decisive and determined approach when assessing and preparing to make a putt. You will save yourself time by having fewer putts to make. The ability to read the green, together with your practiced and trusted putting routine will promote self-confidence, consistency and successful outcomes more often.

CHIPPING

A chip shot is usually played from just off and around the green, where the ground between you and the hole is clear of any hazard or major undulation preventing a suitable roll of the ball.

The golf ball will be in the air initially and then roll forward along the ground towards your target. The shot will be played in such a way as to minimise the amount of backspin upon the ball.

Minimising the amount of backspin upon the golf ball is achieved by leaving out conscious wrist action and creating a shallower arc of the club head as a result.

The less the loft on the club, the less time the ball will be in the air and the more it will roll along the ground. The more the loft on the club, the more time the ball will be in the air and the less it will roll along the ground.

Ensure that the lie and shaft length of your Irons are suitable for you. The sole of each of your Iron clubs should sit level on level ground. You can then be confident that your Irons will perform well when used with care and precision.

To save shots it can be beneficial to be clear in your mind just how the golf ball will react to your stroke. For example, the distance the ball covers in the air, the trajectory of the ball, its reaction upon landing, and the distance and direction of its roll. This reaction will of course differ depending on the Iron club you choose, and how you use it. You can gain this knowledge and become more skilled at this aspect of the game through thoughtful practice, experimentation with your clubs and by gaining more experience out on the golf course.

Your hold for chipping can be your usual iron club hold, or a version of your putter hold. Experiment, and find the best solution that works for you.

You may prefer to use to use, say an 8 or 9 Iron, for

shots that require less roll, and a 5 or 6 Iron for shots requiring more roll. For the average golfer you may initially prefer to practice and build your chipping game around using only two clubs. This can help to build your confidence in this aspect of your game.

During practice, hold the golf ball in your hand and pretend to toss the ball underarm to the target point. Then actually toss the golf ball to the target point and watch the ball roll towards the target. This will help you to gain a good feel for distance and the art of chipping the ball the correct distance towards the hole.

During actual play, prior to playing a chip shot, try pretending to throw the golf ball underarm towards your target, leaving the golf ball where it lies of course. Then rehearse the shot you want to play with your golf club in your hands. This will help you to gain a feel for the weight of the shot. This need not be a time consuming process. Indeed you are more likely to save shots and time when you become more proficient at chipping the golf ball.

When faced with a chip shot, observe the lie of the golf ball, read the line and see in your minds-eye the type of shot that is likely to be most successful. Then select the Iron club that will give you the required trajectory and roll. With practice and experience, you will instinctively get a feel for the best club to utilise in any given situation.

Before addressing the ball, breathe comfortably in and out, to help you feel more relaxed. Smile, switch on your concentration and then step into your focused chipping routine.

Pick your target point, which may be the hole or a point between your balls current position and the hole, for example a blade of grass or mark in the ground. Then pick an interim target point or site mark within a metre of and in front of the golf ball on the target line. It is important to be as precise as possible here. This will assist you in playing your shot along your chosen target line more successfully, providing the right degree of pace is applied to the ball.

Take up your stance with your feet comfortably close together, maintaining your balance with your feet, knees and hips in a slightly open position. For a chip shot, it is desirable for your weight to be slightly more on your left side. The ball position is best set slightly back of centre. There will naturally be very little conscious body movement during the shot.

Your arms hang down naturally and comfortably when playing a chip shot, the arms swing back in a controlled yet comfortable way. The club head goes back fractionally and quite naturally inside the target line.

For a chip shot your hands need to be slightly ahead of the ball at address with the shaft of the golf club forming a straight line with your left arm. This is assisted by just letting the club sit where it was made to sit. Your hands must be comfortably in control and lead the club through the ball.

When placing the club head of your Iron behind the ball at address, the club face (the leading edge when using an Iron) needs to be precisely square to your chosen site mark, with your shoulders parallel to this target line. This is in order to set the golf ball off on the desired path. You can then concentrate on your personal tempo and the pace of the shot. Also, if you can select a fairly flat landing point for your golf ball to land upon this can help you to achieve your objective.

When you play a chip shot, the pace of the shot is governed by the length (back and through) of your 'mini swing'. The club head should be taken back just enough so that the best possible tempo and pace is applied to the shot. You can also experiment by 'choking down' on the grip of the club, even on to the shaft itself where you feel that extra control of the club head is helpful. This is a term used where your hold on the club is further, 'by degrees' down the grip/shaft of the golf club.

Maintain control and an even pace throughout the shot, generally the length of your backswing on a chip shot will match the follow through. There will be a smooth transition back and forth, with the arms pulling the hands and club head through smoothly and naturally from slightly inside the target line.

Your head is over the ball on a chip shot, with your eyes focused on the back of the golf ball, even a dimple to be super precise. There will be a little wrist movement created naturally during the swing of your arms. Avoid any conscious action on your part to stiffen up your wrists or increase your wrist action. However, should you have a poor lie, breaking your wrists by degrees, can help the club into and through the ball. This can be more beneficial to the shot. The aim is to strike the ball slightly before the bottom of the swing arc of the club. This promotes a slightly downward strike on the ball, avoids scooping and creates a crisper shot.

The aim of a chip shot is to promote precision and control, with the club head taken back and accelerating steadily and smoothly through the ball at an even pace. Your natural tempo ensues and the club head follows through straight towards the target.

These pre-shot strategies can 'free you up' to just be in the moment and to be confident and comfortable playing the shot. In essence you have developed a pre-shot routine you can trust, to enable you to move the ball towards the hole successfully. Whatever the outcome, accept it. 'That's Golf'. You have done your best, just move on to the next shot.

PITCHING

A pitch shot is played where there is a hazard and/or undulation in the ground, between your ball and the target, preventing a suitable roll of the golf ball.

The golf ball will be in the air most of the way to the target. It will stop close to where it lands. The shot will be played in such a way so as to impart the desired amount of backspin on the ball.

Backspin is achieved by creating a steeper swing, back, down and forward through the ball, achieved with plenty of wrist action.

You play a pitch shot using the most lofted Irons in your bag, for example the 9 Iron and a variety of wedges.

The pitch shot can be played anywhere from around 130yds out to a position very close to the green.

Ensure that the lie of your Irons and length of shaft are suitable for you. It is ideal if the sole of each of your Iron clubs sit level on level ground at your address position. You can then be confident that your Irons will perform well when used with care and precision.

To save shots and to achieve consistency, establish how far the ball will travel when you play your various pitching clubs. You can only achieve this through practice and experience.

During practice, experiment with your pitching clubs. You may initially prefer to practice and build confidence around one or two clubs, for example the 9 Iron and/or the wedge. Also experiment by 'choking down', by degrees, your hold on the club (moving your hold down the grip/shaft of the club).Try a crisper tempo and vary the length of swing, keeping your personal smooth rhythm, thus applying more backspin to the ball. Discover how this affects the ball in terms of its distance, trajectory, its reaction upon landing and the amount and direction of roll. Also experiment, by degrees, with different ball positions within your stance.

Imagine how good you can become, playing shots into and around the greens. This can also help you when you are in an 'in between clubs' situation out on the course, giving you more shot options.

Before playing a short pitch shot, try this. Pretend to throw an imaginary golf ball under arm towards the target a couple of times. This will help you to gain a feel for the pace and distance of the shot. Then rehearse the shot a couple of times with the Iron club in your hands. This is not time consuming, on the contrary, you will save shots and time by seeing an improvement in your pitching and getting the ball more consistently closer to the hole.

When faced with a pitch shot look at the lie of the golf ball, read the line and see in your imagination the type of shot that is required. Then select the golf club that can produce the ideal trajectory and roll on the golf ball. With practice and experience, you will instinctively get a feel for the best club to use in any given situation.

Before addressing the golf ball breathe comfortably in and slowly out, releasing any unnecessary tension. Smile, then step into your trusted pitching routine. Breathe out gently before you start your takeaway.

From behind the ball, pick your target point, which may be the hole, or a point between your golf balls current position and the hole. Then pick an interim target site mark within a metre of, and in front of the ball, on the target line.

Align the bottom edge (the leading edge) of the Iron club face square to your chosen site mark. You need to be precise here. This will help you to play the shot along your chosen target line more successfully. It is important to know how far you can comfortable play the golf ball with each of your short irons without excessive force, including your wedges. Play within your current capabilities, control is the 'main aim of the game' here. The natural turn of your chest in conjunction with the swinging motion of your arms feels natural and controlled. Your club head will swing back slightly on the inside quite naturally, then down and through to the target. Over swinging is to be avoided, and this is helped by adopting a slightly open stance (whilst maintaining the club on line). This will naturally curb somewhat, any tendency to over swing. Also this set up imparts more spin on the golf ball which aids control.

The distance of the shot, produced by the Iron club you have chosen, has a direct correlation to the length of your back swing and playing within yourself. The whole process should feel unforced and comfortable in order to achieve consistency and success.

When pitching, always keep your hands leading the club into and through the ball at impact. This is best achieved by combining early cocking of the wrists, with a controlled turn of your chest. You swing down decisively and crisply letting this feel natural to you. Your narrower stance, and the natural position of your head as a result of this, will quite naturally create a more down and through swing, so do not overdo this action, just let it be. The wrists stay cocked until quite late in the down swing.

The use of more lofted wedges around the green is challenging to the average player, with the possibility of thinning the shot and the consequences that can bring. More advanced players may develop different techniques, possibly with more lofted wedges. Opening and closing the clubface to various degrees, leading more, or less, with the hands, and/or increasing hand hold pressure, 'by degrees' individually or together. Also trying different ball positions and creating different responses from the golf ball. However, learning to acquire these skills, will have taken much time and practice to achieve. Play within your current capabilities when out on the course.

The pitch shot follow through is shorter than your backswing. Nevertheless, you hold your finish, and see the result of the shot you have created.

Putting is a continual learning process.

BUNKER PLAY

The main objective of your bunker play is to get the golf ball out of the bunker on the first attempt, and to move the golf ball as close to the flag as possible when around the green.

You can develop your skills, by learning and practicing the techniques for any given situation, and enjoying this aspect of the game.

Through thoughtful practice and play, you can gain more and more skill and experience in bunker play. It is important therefore for you to develop your own reliable and trusted routine for bunker shots. This can bring you more consistency and accomplishment in this area of the game.

The rules of golf do allow your golf club to be grounded away from the ball in a bunker. However you cannot ground your club when playing a bunker shot. If you do, then you incur a penalty.

To get a feel for the density and workability of the sand, you do so using your feet. As you gauge this, you are steadily grinding down and feeling your feet form a solid foundation for your swing. This prevents unhelpful sinking and sliding of the feet during the shot. Your weight, by degrees, is best set slightly more on your left side but do not overdo this.

The ideal scenario is for your golf swing to allow the club head to hit the sand around two inches behind the ball on a standard shot. You position your head so that your eyes are focused over this spot. The ball position is best set further forward 'by degrees' in your stance and the grip of the club will naturally be positioned further back than normal.

You then tailor the length of your swing to the length of shot required. You adjust the amount of speed and power applied to control the amount of backspin upon the ball. You can even experiment where required by 'choking down' on the grip/ shaft of the club. You can see how important good technique and practice are in the area of bunker play.

With comfortably flexed knees, you align your feet, comfortably open, 'by degrees', to the left of your chosen target line. The bottom edge of your sand wedge is aligned towards the target away from the ball, before assembling your light yet firm hold on the grip. This opens the face of the club to promote a cutting action which is ideal.

You will notice that as your sand wedge is more open this brings the flange (known as the bounce of the club) more into play preventing the club head from digging into the sand. You are effectively playing the shot with the bounce, which allows the clubface to glide through the sand under the ball. The softer the sand, the more open, by degrees, you stand and the more open the clubface will be. Also your weight in these circumstances is best spread evenly across your stance.

You maintain a light firm hold on the club to facilitate a relaxed feeling in your forearms and wrists. You incorporate an early wrist break just after takeaway in your backswing. By setting your wrists early, this will help you to achieve a natural feeling of controlled power. You maintain the angle created by leading the downswing with your left hand, accelerating through the sand and releasing your right hand as the golf ball sets off on its way to your chosen target. Your right arm then straightens.

Remember, you are swinging the club along the line of your feet. The bottom edge (the leading edge) of the club head will be aimed at your chosen target. Also, because of the cutting action that naturally results in this set up, you aim slightly left of your target. This is because the golf ball will have a tendency to spin left to right when it lands.

Some bunkers consist of a harder under layer with a covering of sand with little depth to it. In some instances the sand in a bunker is wet and heavier in consistency. When presented with these different situations your technique changes to help you achieve your objective. Given these circumstances the flange of your sand wedge, so useful in soft sand, is taken out of play. This will help you to control the shot, by preventing the flange from bouncing off the harder surface in the bunker. You achieve this by squaring up the bottom leading edge of the club face to your chosen target away from the ball. You swing the club as you would for a normal wedge shot with your weight favouring your left side. Your golf ball will leave the bunker on a lower trajectory and roll forward more upon landing, so bear this in mind. When applying a little more force you can go for the hole to allow for the effect of backspin on the golf ball. An alternative is to use a wedge with less bounce or a standard pitching wedge.

Again correct technique, practice and gaining experience are the keys to your improvement. This will enable you to really enjoy bunker play. The variety of shots within your capability can increase your enjoyment and satisfaction in this area of the game. This can also save you shots and increase your confidence as a result.

Where you are faced with an uphill lie you remember to adjust the line of your shoulders to the slope. Your weight will naturally be more on your right side, with your right knee comfortable flexed. You realise that the golf ball will travel less far, on a higher trajectory, so that it may require more momentum to reach your chosen target. You may even consider using a less lofted wedge. Where the upslope is at a greater angle you naturally bend your left knee, 'by degrees' to give you a more solid and comfortable stance. Also you will aim a little more right of your target to help to compensate for a tendency to move the ball right to left.

CHRISTOPHER PEAKE

When faced with a downhill lie, again you can adjust the line of your shoulders to the slope. You can open the clubface slightly and have the golf ball a little further back in your stance. Set the right hand wrist cock early, and as it releases through the ball, chase your right hand down the slope. Your finish position is lower and somewhat curtailed. The trajectory of the ball will be lower with more forward roll. Where the down slope is at a greater angle you naturally bend your right knee, 'by degrees' to allow you to be more solid and comfortable. You may also consider 'choking down' on the grip of the club. Also you will aim a little more left of your target to help to compensate for a tendency to move the ball left to right.

Where the golf ball is partially buried in the sand, you play the shot with a square clubface and play the ball like a normal wedge shot. You play the shot steadily as the trajectory of the golf ball will be lower, with more forward roll upon landing.

Where the ball is more deeply buried, you can slightly close the club face. Your stance will be nearer to square to the line of the shot. The golf ball can be a little further back in your stance, if you prefer, but do not overdo this. Your weight will be more on your left side. You aim for the back of the plug/ball with a solid steady swing. The trajectory of the golf ball will be low followed by a lot of forward momentum as the ball rolls onwards. You can of course opt for a wedge with less bounce instead.

Where the golf ball is below your feet in a bunker, the shot you play will tend to, 'by degrees' move left to right. To help to counteract this you align yourself, 'by degrees' to the left of the target. Focus on maintaining your posture and hit through the sand.

Where your golf ball is above your feet in a bunker the shot you play will tend to, 'by degrees' move right to left. So align yourself, 'by degrees' to the right. Choke down the grip of the club slightly to compensate for the slope of the ground. Then play your shot steadily and surely to your chosen target.

FAIRWAY AND LONG BUNKER SHOTS

When faced with a longer bunker shot, for example a fairway bunker, you will realise that using a sand wedge may not be the most useful option, in terms of gaining some distance towards the green. However getting out of the bunker successfully is your most important objective, so use your judgement and course management skills and play the shot within your current capabilities.

The position and quality of the lie of your golf ball will be a major factor when determining your strategy for the shot. The aim is to get out of the bunker so, as we have said, it is best practice to play within your current capabilities. Concentrate upon keeping your balance and pick the right club for you to achieve that objective.

Learn about the texture of the sand through your feet, as with any bunker play. Gain a sound footing you can rely on, with your weight evenly spread across your slightly open stance. Maintain a good posture, focus on the back of the ball, swing smoothly and steadily and lead with your left hand.

Take less sand, by hitting more into the back of the golf ball which can be a little further back in your stance depending upon your personal preference. Keep your body steadily balanced and swing your arms with a steady rhythm. In some instances you may feel it necessary to open the clubface 'by degrees' to help to negotiate the lip of a bunker successfully. Also, you can where necessary 'choke down' on the grip of the club, to compensate for the depth of your feet in the sand.

Your control of distance is governed by the length of your swing and the controlled acceleration of the club into and through the ball. The direction is determined by the club face being square to the target line.

Bunker play is an integral part of the game of golf. Practice when you can, and as you gain experience on the golf course, your confidence and skill in this aspect of your game can improve.

GETTING OUT
OF THE ROUGH

When your golf ball is in the rough be realistic and stay calm. Observe the lie of your ball and plan your shot from that viewpoint. Do not go for distance at the expense of getting the ball out of the situation. Play within your current capabilities. When in this situation, have the golf ball further back in your stance to help to encourage a more descending swing arc into the ball. Open the clubface, by degrees, to counteract any tendency for the club head to close. This is caused by the effect of the grass on the head and shaft of the golf club. The deeper the rough the more open the clubface can be. Indeed, circumstances may dictate that you play the shot as if you were in the sand, opening the club face and taking the grass and ball. Be careful however, where you are aiming. Think about maintaining good balance and posture and hitting the golf ball crisply.In lighter rough, depending upon the lie of your ball, you may be able to just play a relatively normal shot.

LIE OF THE LAND SLOPING UPWARDS

Where you are faced with an uphill lie adjust the line of your shoulders to the slope, and play the ball, 'by degrees' further back in your stance. Your golf ball will not travel as far and will travel on a higher trajectory, so consider that you may require a longer club to reach your chosen target.

Where the upslope is at a greater angle you naturally bend your left knee, 'by degrees' to give you a more solid and comfortable stance.

Also you can aim a little more to the right of your target to help to compensate for a tendency to move the ball right to left.

LIE OF THE LAND SLOPING DOWNWARDS

When faced with a downhill lie, again you adjust the line of your shoulders to the slope. You can open the clubface slightly and have the golf ball a little further back than normal in your stance. The trajectory of the ball will be lower with more forward roll, so you may, depending on the circumstances choose to select a shorter club for the shot.

Where the down slope is at a greater angle you naturally bend your right knee, 'by degrees' to allow you to feel more solid and comfortable with the shot. You can aim a little more left of your target to help to compensate for a tendency to move the ball left to right.

BALL ABOVE
YOUR FEET

You will notice that, with the golf ball above your feet, you quite naturally stand a little more upright. The ball is, 'by degrees' further away from your feet. Also the ball is played around the centre of your centre balanced stance. This will create conditions contributing to a flatter swing plane, coupled with a tendency to create a right to left ball flight.

You bring into your set up a 'choking down' of your hold on the grip of the golf club.

To help you deal with these circumstances, you bend from your waist, 'by degrees' and choke down on the golf club. You judge the amount of bend and choke down, by degrees, depending upon the amount of slope that you are dealing with. The greater the slope the more compensation you will make.

Your turn will be somewhat restricted, so overturning is to be avoided, giving more emphasis on your balance and a more compact action. Make a steady, smooth and controlled swing and put the golf ball in a good place for your next shot.

You may feel it advisable to take a longer club to compensate for the loss of distance this set up produces. Again play within your current capabilities and select a club that you feel confident with. Put the golf ball in a good playing position for your next shot.

Lastly and importantly open the club face a little, by degrees, and aim, by degrees, to the right of your chosen target. This will help to compensate for the right to left ball flight that these conditions bring about.

Always play within your current capabilities, and as you gain more skill and experience your confidence will improve.

BALL BELOW
YOUR FEET

In contrast to the ball above your feet scenario, in this situation you find yourself quite naturally bending more from your waist and flexing your knees. You will also notice that your golf ball is closer to your feet. This will create conditions contributing to a more upright swing coupled with a tendency to move the golf ball left to right.

Hold the golf club comfortably at the top of the grip to help you to stand a, little taller.

Your swing and follow through will be somewhat restricted. Widen your stance by degrees and avoid overturning. Give more emphasis on your balance and a smooth, steady and compact swing action, to a balanced finish.

You may feel it advisable to take a longer club to compensate for the loss of distance this set up produces. Again play within your current capabilities and put the golf ball in a good position for your next shot.

Lastly and importantly close the club face a little, by degrees, and aim, by degrees, to the left of your chosen target. This will help to compensate for the movement of the golf ball from left to right that these conditions bring about.

Again, always play within your current capabilities, as you gain more skill and experience, so your confidence will improve.

ON COURSE STRATEGY

It is essential that you manage yourself well from within, in order to make sound strategic decisions whilst out on the golf course. Think and work out your thoughts and actions back from the green to the tee. This will help you make the right choices for you, in terms of where on the tee you set up your golf ball and your target landing area for the shot in hand.

It is important to know how far you can send your golf ball with each club in your bag. You will appreciate that this takes time to develop, especially if you are new to the game. However you can do this with commitment, patience and practice, however it is important that you are practicing the right techniques in order for you to make progress. For example your posture, and the way in which you stand, align yourself to the target and hold the golf club. With this in mind, investing in a few lessons with a professional is a good idea to start you off on your golfing journey. By starting off on a sound footing, this will help you to make steady progress towards achieving your individual potential.

An essential for good strategy is planning your round, if you know the golf course this is helped by your 'local knowledge'. Otherwise a course planner, if available, is advantageous. You can decide in principle which clubs you aim to utilise on each hole taking account of any hazards and the standard of your golf game at the time. Play within your current capabilities and distances that you can comfortably achieve. Let your improvement in the game take its natural course.

Other essentials are to know the distance of your target from your present position, judging the lie of the land and prevailing weather conditions. If the ground is dry and hard the golf ball will roll forward on landing. If conditions are heavier then there will be less forward momentum of the ball.

Knowing where on the course various challenges

are, can help you to plan your shots, to minimise future shot difficulty. For instance where a par three hole has an elevated tee, possibly requiring a shorter club than usual, or where a par three has an elevated green, possibly requiring a longer club. You can also make any adjustments necessary for the prevailing conditions.

When playing your shots always pick a specific target point, especially when playing from the tee to the fairway.

Imagine that you are on the tee for a moment. If the lie of the land presented to you slopes left to right or right to left, assess to what extent this may affect the golf ball upon landing.

Now imagine that there are hazards on the low side, heavy rough, trees or even out of bounds. You have to make decisive sound common sense decisions for you depending upon your current level of play. Consider the following actions. Play a fade or a draw into the slope remembering to pick a precise target. If a fade or draw shot is not currently in your armoury, then play your natural swing and compensate by moving your target, and your alignment, by degrees, left or right. You could opt for playing a higher shot to lessen the roll of the golf ball upon landing.

When teeing up your golf ball, remember that the teeing area is two club lengths deep from the line between the tee markers. Pick a good flat spot that you like to give you a good feeling about the shot in hand, and that gives you as sounder footing as possible. Also if you tee up behind a divot mark, for example, on a par three hole, pick one that is pointing directly to the target to help with your alignment.

When fairway bunkers feature on a hole it usually pays you to drive over them from the tee if this is within your capability. This potentially leaves you with a shorter shot into the green with better hold upon landing. Laying up short of a fairway bunker may be the better option for some players. Subsequently play the ball into the best possible position for a good shot into the green.

Some golfers have a natural tendency to draw or fade the golf ball and this can be helpful when playing a hole that dog-legs left or right. You can benefit from this by having a target line straight down the middle of the fairway from the tee and allowing your natural action to fade or draw the ball.

When playing a dog-leg, unless you have a draw or

fade shot that you are confident in, it is best to go down the middle. Take a shorter wood or an iron club if you are going to run out of fairway and end up in heavy rough or trees.

If you try to play the shot to close to the corner of the dog-leg you leave little margin for error and can end up losing shots as a result. So always give yourself the best chance of success on this type of hole, play within yourself and your current capabilities.

When working on your game in respect of your ability to move the golf ball left or right, teeing the ball lower will assist you with a fade shot and teeing the ball higher will assist you in bringing off a draw. Using a three wood, with its higher loft, rather than a driver, will help you to launch the ball when playing the draw. This is because the action that takes place during the swing closes the club face into and through the ball. Persevere and practice, and you will be spurred on and enjoy the variety of shots you are able to make, and strengthen your game as a result.

When playing a shot into the green go for the centre of the green unless, having assessed the situation and the challenges the hole presents to you, you feel able to go for the flag. Play within your current capabilities. The aim is to put yourself in the best possible situation minimising the degree of difficulty for your next shot. The situation may be such that you decide to lay the ball up in front of the green, and then get up and down from there.

Another factor is the lie of your golf ball, how it is sitting on the turf. Where the ground is hard and bare and the best option is a wedge shot, play the ball comfortably by degrees back in your stance, open the club face, by degrees and focus on the back of the ball. Keep your head steady, your hands will naturally be a little further forward.

If the lie is poor, then play for the centre of the green. If you are able to move the ball left or right on landing then go for the fat part of the green and work the ball left or right as required to the flag. If you are not at that advanced stage with your game then just go for the centre of the green, relying on your putting skills to get the ball in the hole.

When your golf ball has come to rest in a divot, choking down the grip slightly can give you a feeling of more control and confidence. Concentrate on swinging down and through the divot, again keeping your head steady.

Imagine that there is a mound between you and the green and you are fairly close to the green. An option is to bump the golf ball into the bank and let it bounce up and onto the putting surface. However be aware that conditions in terms of any grass or wet ground can mean that this type of shot is not the best option. Use your best judgement at the time. Also remember the slope and contours of the green will have an effect on the golf ball after landing on the putting surface, as will the direction of the grain.

Leaving yourself with the best possible putt is the best outcome that you are looking to achieve. Avoid situations involving subsequent downhill putts moving away from you which, although can be made, are very tricky.

When you are playing a shot into a green that slopes from back to front, crafting a 'punch shot' is often the best option. Play the golf ball a little further back and narrow your stance. This is also an option when playing into a two tier green where the flag is towards the rear of the top tier. Going for the flag in these circumstances can result in the ball bouncing forward off the back of the green!

There may be circumstances where you would normally play a particular short iron (a nine iron for instance) into a green sloping from back to front. You realise that the backspin created will encourage the golf ball to roll down the putting surface, and maybe even roll off the green entirely! The best option here could be to play a less lofted club (say an eight iron). You then hold the golf club further down the grip of the club (known as 'choking down in the game') and feel a little less pressure in your hands. Swing the club nice and steady in order to reduce the amount of back spin upon the ball. This helps the ball to 'stay put' as much as possible upon landing. Of course, the degree of slope, together with your current golfing ability, will affect the strategy you adopt in any given situation.

Again, spending a little time on 'the punch shot' in practice sessions can help to develop your skills and potentially save you shots out on the golf course.

Where you are near to the green and there is a bunker between you and the hole, you could try the 'floater shot' having the ball further forward and widening your stance. The ball lands softly on the green with little forward roll. This also works well when playing to a green higher up than your current position.

When you are playing into the wind, you can adopt, by degrees, a wider stance to help you to keep your balance. Play within yourself, and play the ball a little further back in your stance. Slow down your normal swing, keeping your arms relaxed, thus encouraging the golf ball to spin less during its flight. Let your right hand release through the ball and your right arm roll and straighten towards the target, followed by a balanced finish. Also you can use a stronger club than normal to compensate for this and the prevailing conditions.

When you are playing with the wind off the tee, strive to keep your balance and swing with a nice rhythm at a steady tempo. Do not be tempted to force the issue to gain more distance. If you are playing your driver off the tee the ball will not fly so high. This is because the wind will counteract the normal trajectory, so you can go with a three wood and you will get good results. Also take account of any hazards that could be brought into play when deciding your strategy.

When you are playing from the fairway to the green, with the wind behind you, take a club with lesser loft to compensate for this. It is best to keep the ball low using the 'Punch shot' playing the ball further back in a narrower stance, with your weight around twenty percent more on your left side. Using a three quarter backswing, transfer down and through the ball, punching it forward on a lower trajectory. This affords you more control than leaving the golf ball to the mercy of the wind by flying it high.

When you are playing in cross winds the best scenario for most players is to adjust the target line accordingly and allow the wind to play its part in the shot. More advanced players who are able to move the ball left or right have more options. Stay solid and swing within yourself. Play within your current level of ability,

During wet weather play, go with your fairway woods or utility clubs, as long irons become more of a challenge. This is especially so for the average player, even if you have to 'choke down' the shaft of the club in some situations. You will achieve better control and results on the day.

When putting in wet weather, the extra moisture on the green means that the roll of the golf ball will slow down much sooner than in dry conditions. You have to compensate for this by applying more forward momentum to the ball. Leaving the ball short is not an option. Also a breaking putt will not break as much in wet conditions. You will become more accustomed to these situations as you gain experience.

Remember to play within your current capabilities. Practice thoughtfully and gain experience, by adopting well thought out strategies and your game will naturally improve.

FINAL
THOUGHTS

Play within your current capabilities and enjoy practicing methodically to develop your ability in the various aspects of the game. Ingrain the basics, gain more skill and experience. You can then quite naturally become more creative, your confidence will rise, enhancing your fulfilment and enjoyment of the game.

Remember a small change can make a big difference.

It is my sincere wish that the information contained in

this book will **enable you** to

experience and reach your full golfing potential.

Thank you for reading

Printed in Great Britain
by Amazon

19714259R00078